The Usborne
Very First
Dictionary
in French

Felicity Brooks, Caroline Young and Claire Masset
Designed by Francesca Allen and Keith Newell
Illustrated by Jo Litchfield

Contents

2 A–Z dictionary
58 Where are they?
60 I, you, he, she
61 Questions
62 Colours, shapes, numbers
64 Months, days, seasons
65 Using your dictionary
68 French word list

Here are some children you will meet in this book.

Ellie   Ben   Molly   Polly Jack   Robert   Laura   Olly Emily

You can hear all the French words in this book, read by a French person, on the
Usborne Quicklinks Website at **www.usborne-quicklinks.com** Find out more on page 80.

A

afternoon
l'après-midi (m)

a sunny **afternoon**
un **après-midi** ensoleillé

all
tout (m), toute (f), tous, toutes

They are **all** playing music.
Ils jouent **tous** de la musique.

about — sur

He reads a book **about** school.

Il lit un livre **sur** l'école.

again — encore

The little girl bounces, and bounces **again**.

La petite fille bondit, et bondit **encore**.

alphabet
l'alphabet (m)

abcdefgh ijklmnopq rstuvwxyz

after — après

one **after** the other

l'une **après** l'autre

air — l'air (m), les airs

Balloons float in the **air**.

Les montgolfières volent dans les **airs**.

always — toujours

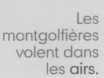

Tom **always** wears socks.

Tom met **toujours** des chaussettes.

ambulance
l'ambulance (f)

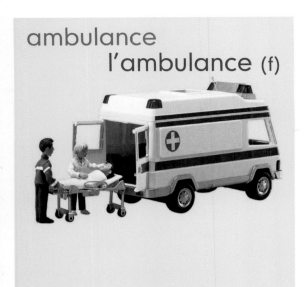

animal
l'animal (m), les animaux

some farm animals

des animaux de la ferme

ant
la fourmi

some ants   des fourmis

angel
l'ange (m)

ankle
la cheville

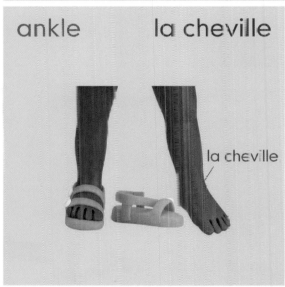

la cheville

any
du (m), de la (f), des (plural)

Is there any soup?

Est-ce qu'il y a de la soupe ?

angry
fâché

This girl looks angry.

Cette fille a l'air fâché.

another
encore

Danny wants another lemonade.

Danny veut encore une limonade.

apple
la pomme

A
B

are | sont

The monkeys **are** brown.

Les singes **sont** marron.

asleep | endormi

Shhh! The little boy's **asleep**.

Chut ! Le petit garçon est **endormi**.

Bb

arm | le bras

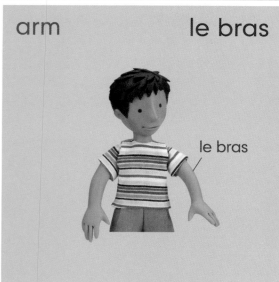

le bras

astronaut
l'astronaute (m/f)

baby | le bébé

ask | demander

The girl **asks** who's on the phone.

La fille **demande** qui est à l'appareil.

awake | éveillé, réveillé

They are still **awake**.

Ils sont encore **éveillés**.

bad | mauvais

The apple tastes **bad**.

La pomme a **mauvais** goût.

bag   le sac

banana   la banane

beach   la plage

ball   le ballon, la balle

basket   le panier

bear   l'ours (m)

balloon   le ballon

three **balloons**   trois **ballons**

bath   le bain

She is having a bath.   Elle prend un bain.

bed   le lit

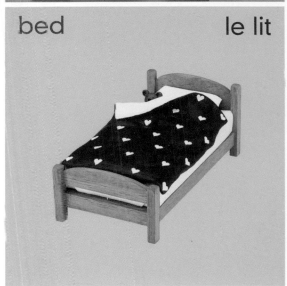

5

bee l'abeille (f)

big grand

Swans are big birds.

Les cygnes sont de grands oiseaux.

bite la bouchée

The boy is taking a bite.

Le garçon prend une bouchée.

belt la ceinture

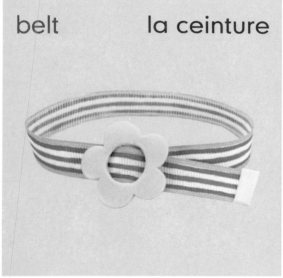

bird l'oiseau (m), les oiseaux

blanket la couverture

bicycle la bicyclette, le vélo

birthday l'anniversaire (m)

a birthday cake
un gâteau d'anniversaire

boat le bateau, les bateaux

bone   l'os (m), les os

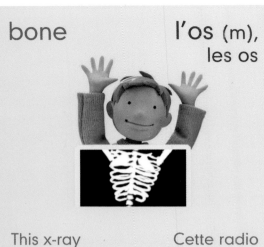

This x-ray shows the boy's bones.   Cette radio montre les os du garçon.

bowl   le bol

The bowl is full.   Le bol est plein.

bread   le pain

book   le livre

box   la boîte

breakfast   le petit déjeuner

boots   les bottes (f)

boy   le garçon

brother   le frère

two brothers   deux frères

brush   la brosse

butterfly   le papillon

Cc

build   construire

The men build a wall.

Les hommes construisent un mur.

button   le bouton

some buttons   des boutons

cake   le gâteau,
les gâteaux

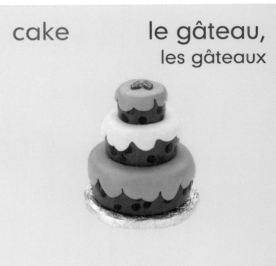

bus   l'autobus (m),
le bus

buy   acheter

He is buying
a lollipop.

Il achète une sucette.

can   pouvoir

How many girls can you see?

Tu peux voir combien de filles ?

car   la voiture

cat   le chat

cheese   le fromage

carrot   la carotte

two carrots   deux carottes

catch   attraper

"Catch!" says the boy.

"Attrape !" dit le garçon.

cherry   la cerise

red cherries   des cerises rouges

castle   le château,
les châteaux

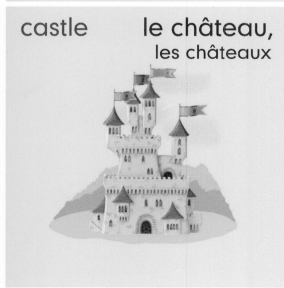

chair   la chaise

chicken   le poulet

two chickens   deux poulets

chocolate **le chocolat**

cloud **le nuage**

come **venir**

The clown **comes** to Luke's house.

Le clown **vient** chez Luke.

clock **la pendule**

coat **le manteau,** les manteaux

computer **l'ordinateur** (m)

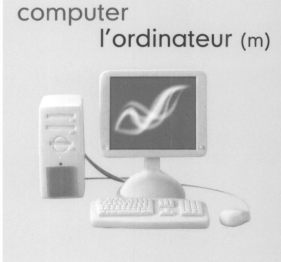

clothes **les vêtements** (m)

warm **clothes**

des **vêtements** chauds

cold **froid**

It's **cold** in winter.

Il fait **froid** en hiver.

cook **faire la cuisine**

Sam **cooks**. Sam **fait la cuisine**.

cow — la vache

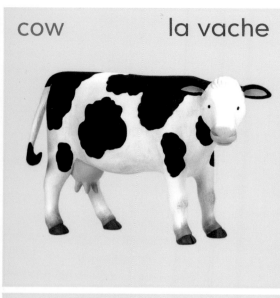

cry — pleurer

The little boy is crying.
Le petit garçon pleure.

cup — la tasse

Dd

dance — danser

This girl loves to dance.

Cette fille aime danser.

dark — noir

It's dark outside.

Il fait noir dehors.

day — le jour

The sun rises every day.

Le soleil se lève tous les jours.

deep — profond

Diggers make deep holes.

Les pelleteuses font des trous profonds.

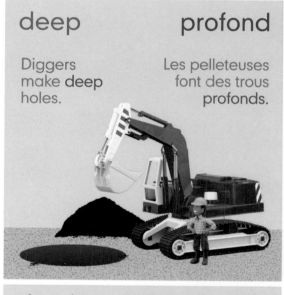

dentist — le/la dentiste

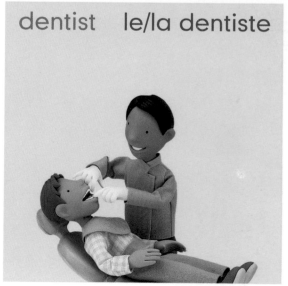

dig **creuser**

Anna is digging a hole.

Anna creuse un trou.

dirty **sale**

The digger is dirty.

La pelleteuse est sale.

dog **le chien**

digger **la pelleteuse**

do **faire**

There's lots to do at the beach.

Il y a beaucoup à faire à la plage.

doll **la poupée**

dinosaur **le dinosaure**

doctor **le médecin, le docteur**

donkey **l'âne** (m)

| door | la porte | dress | la robe | drum | le tambour |

door — la porte

dress — la robe

drum — le tambour
This boy is playing a drum.

Ce garçon joue du tambour.

dragon — le dragon

drink — la boisson

a cold drink   une boisson fraîche

dry — sec (m), sèche (f)

The washing is dry.

Le linge est sec.

draw — dessiner

This girl likes drawing.

Cette fille aime dessiner.

drive — conduire
This woman drives a red car.

Cette femme conduit une voiture rouge.

duck — le canard

Ee

ear   l'oreille (f)

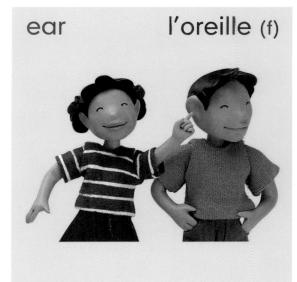

egg   l'œuf (m)

three eggs   trois œufs

each   chaque

Each child   Chaque enfant
has a toy.   a un jouet.

Earth   la Terre

elbow   le coude

le coude

eagle   l'aigle (m)

eat   manger

This boy   Ce garçon
is eating   mange des
pasta.   pâtes.

elephant
l'éléphant (m)

empty — vide

The bath is empty.

La baignoire est vide.

Ff

family — la famille

end — le bout

There's a girl at each end.

Il y a une fille à chaque bout.

face — le visage

a happy face — un visage souriant

farm — la ferme

eye — l'œil (m), les yeux

fairy — la fée

fast — vite

This car goes very fast.

Cette voiture va très vite.

fat gros (m), grosse (f)

This cat is fat.

Ce chat est **gros**.

fire engine la voiture de pompiers

flag le drapeau, les drapeaux

finger le doigt

le doigt

firefighter le pompier

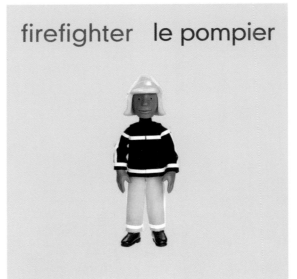

floor le sol

The **floor** is clean.

Le **sol** est propre.

fire le feu

fish le poisson

lots of **fish**   beaucoup de **poissons**

flower la fleur

fly   voler

These birds **are flying**.

Ces oiseaux **volent**.

forest   la forêt

friend   l'ami (m), l'amie (f)

food   la nourriture

fork   la fourchette

frog   la grenouille

foot   le pied

le pied

fox   le renard

fruit   les fruits (m)

Gg

gate   la barrière

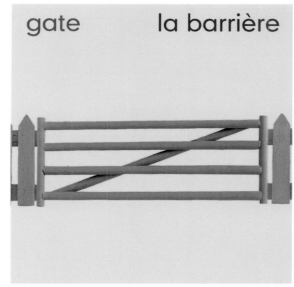

giraffe   la girafe

two **giraffes**   deux **girafes**

game   le jeu, les jeux

ghost   le fantôme

girl   la fille

three **girls**   trois **filles**

garden   le jardin

giant   le géant

give   donner

She **gives** her friend a present.

Elle **donne** un cadeau à son amie.

glass — le verre

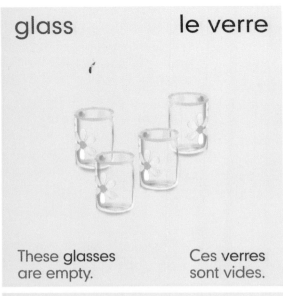

These **glasses** are empty. / Ces **verres** sont vides.

go — aller

This bus **goes** to the supermarket.

Ce bus **va** au supermarché.

goldfish — le poisson rouge

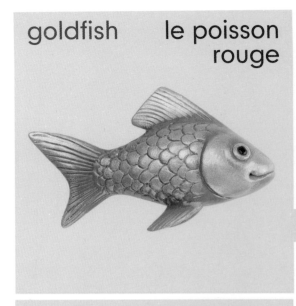

g

glasses — les lunettes (f)

goat — la chèvre

two **goats** / deux **chèvres**

good — bon (m), bonne (f)

These cakes look **good**. / Ces gâteaux ont l'air bon.

gloves — les gants (m)

gold — l'or (m)

goose — l'oie (f)

grapes   le raisin

grow   pousser

These flowers **grow** quickly.

Ces fleurs **poussent** vite.

Hh

grass   l'herbe (f),
la pelouse

grown-up   la grande
personne

a boy and
a **grown-up**

un garçon et
une **grande
personne**

hair   les cheveux (m)

les
cheveux

ground   la terre

The girl falls on the **ground**.

La fille tombe
par **terre**.

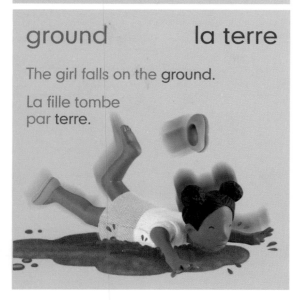

guinea pig   le cochon
d'Inde

hamster   le hamster

hand   la main

la main

hat   le chapeau,
les chapeaux

helicopter
l'hélicoptère (m)

happy   heureux (m),
heureuse (f)

head   la tête

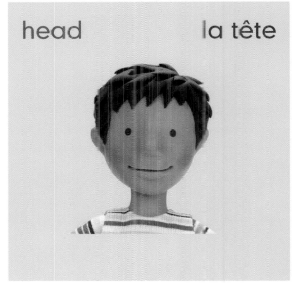

help   aider

The boy **helps**
his dad with
the shopping.

Le garçon **aide**
son papa à
faire les courses.

hard   dur

Stones are
very **hard**.

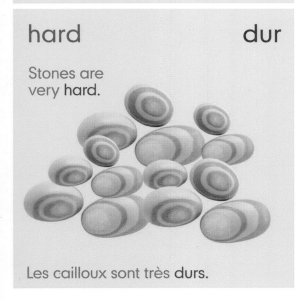

Les cailloux sont très **durs**.

hear   entendre

Jack **hears**
a noise.

Jack **entend**
un bruit.

hide   se cacher

The clown
is hiding.

Le clown
se cache.

hit   frapper

Lucy **hits** the ball.

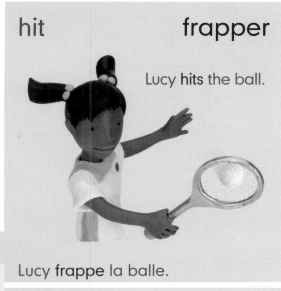

Lucy **frappe** la balle.

honey   le miel

horse   le cheval, les chevaux

hole   le trou

This cheese has **holes** in it.

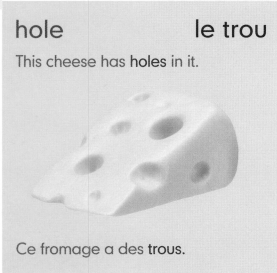

Ce fromage a des **trous**.

hood   la capuche

hospital   l'hôpital (m), les hôpitaux

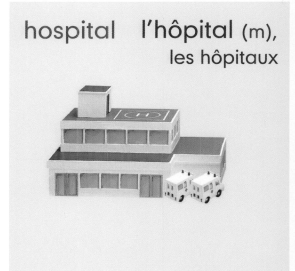

home   la maison

hop   sauter à cloche-pied

Can you hop?

Tu sais **sauter** à cloche-pied ?

hot   chaud

The pans are **hot**.

Les casseroles sont **chaudes**.

house   la maison

hug   embrasser

Olly **hugs** his teddy bear.   Olly **embrasse** son nounours.

hurt   faire mal

Mark's arm **hurts**.

Le bras de Mark lui **fait mal**.

Ii

ice   la glace

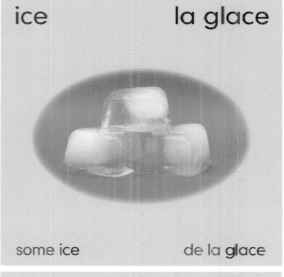

some **ice**   de la **glace**

ice cream   la glace

idea   l'idée (f)

John has an **idea**.   John a une **idée**.

if   si

If you go out, take your umbrella.

Si tu sors, prends ton parapluie.

ink   l'encre (f)

green **ink**

de l'**encre** verte

insect   l'insecte (m)

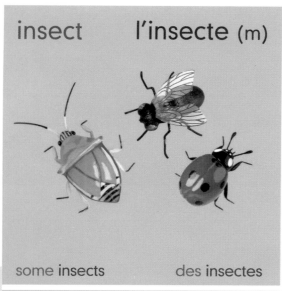

some insects   des insectes

is   est

The soup is delicious.

La soupe est délicieuse.

J j

invitation   l'invitation (f)

Olivia invite
Francesca
à son anniversaire
le 13 février à 3 heures.

island   l'île (f)

jacket   la veste

iron   le fer à repasser

itch   démanger

Fred's ear itches.

L'oreille de Fred le démange.

jar   le pot

two jars of jam   deux pots de confiture

jeans — le jean, les jeans

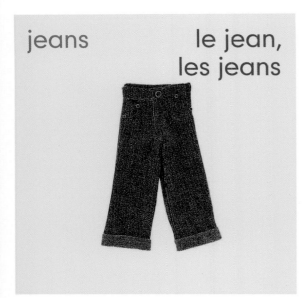

jigsaw puzzle — le puzzle

juice — le jus

jewel — la pierre précieuse

There are jewels in the crown.

Il y a des pierres précieuses sur la couronne.

job — l'emploi (m)

Vicky has a job as a vet.

Vicky a un emploi de vétérinaire.

jump — sauter

One cat jumps off the sofa.

Un chat saute du canapé.

jewellery les bijoux (m)

juggle — jongler

The clown can juggle.

Le clown sait jongler.

jungle — la jungle

i
j

Kk

key   la clé, la clef

kiss   le baiser

His mum gives him a **kiss**.

Sa maman lui donne un **baiser**.

kangaroo
le kangourou

kick   donner un coup de pied

He **kicks** the ball.

Il donne un coup de pied dans le ballon.

kitchen   la cuisine

ketchup   le ketchup

king   le roi

kite   le cerf-volant

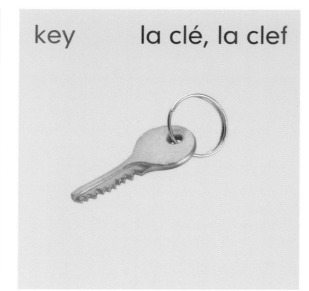

kitten   le chaton

five **kittens**   cinq **chatons**

knee   le genou,
les genoux

— le genou

knife   le couteau,
les couteaux

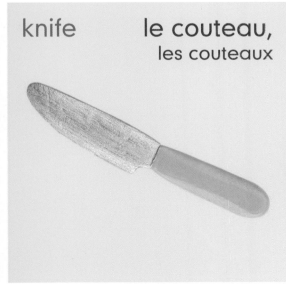

LI

ladybird   la coccinelle

lamb   l'agneau (m),
les agneaux

lamp   la lampe

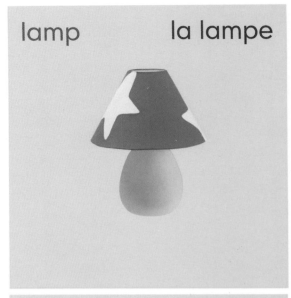

laugh   rire

These children are laughing.   Ces enfants rient.

leaf   la feuille

green **leaves**

des **feuilles** vertes

k
l

leg — **la jambe**

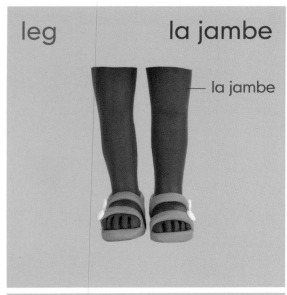

la jambe

letter — **la lettre**

This is the **letter** C.
Voici la **lettre** C.

like — **aimer**

Cats **like** to play.

Les chats aiment jouer.

lemon — **le citron**

three lemons

trois **citrons**

lie — **être couché**

Kirsty is lying in bed.

Kirsty **est couchée** dans le lit.

lion — **le lion**

let — **laisser**

Eve **lets** Bob play with her scooter.

Eve **laisse** Bob jouer avec sa trottinette.

light — **clair**

It's **light** during the day.

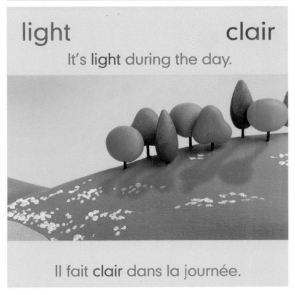

Il fait **clair** dans la journée.

lips — **les lèvres** (f)

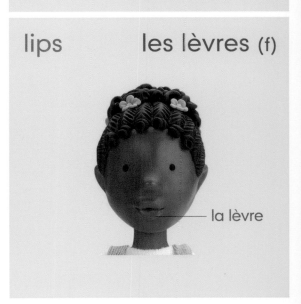

la lèvre

L

listen — écouter

Jack is listening.

Jack écoute.

long — long (m), longue (f)

Amy has long hair.

Amy a les cheveux longs.

loud — fort

WOOF, WOOF!

WOUAH, WOUAH !

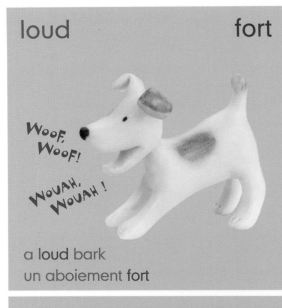

a loud bark
un aboiement fort

little — petit

He's little.

Il est petit.

look (at) — regarder

They are looking at the picture.
Ils regardent l'image.

love — aimer

The children love painting.

Les enfants aiment
faire de la peinture.

live — habiter

A family lives here.

Une famille habite ici.

lots — beaucoup

Spot has lots of puppies.

Spot a beaucoup de chiots.

lunch — le déjeuner

Mm

make   **faire**

They **are making** cakes.   Ils **font** des gâteaux.

mermaid   **la sirène**

machine   **la machine**

a sewing machine   une **machine** à coudre

man   **l'homme** (m)

mess   **le désordre**

magic   **la magie**

map   **la carte**

milk   **le lait**

| mirror | la glace, le miroir | monster | le monstre | morning | le matin |

mirror   la glace, le miroir

monster   le monstre

morning   le matin

a beautiful morning   un beau matin

money   l'argent (m)

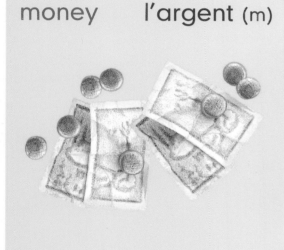

moon   la lune

motorbike   la moto

He's riding a motorbike.   Il fait de la moto.

monkey   le singe

more   plus

Which arm has **more** birds on it?

Sur quel bras y a-t-il **plus** d'oiseaux ?

mountain   la montagne

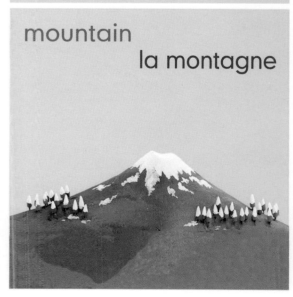

mouse   la souris

mud   la boue

This girl has **mud** on her.   Cette fille a de la **boue** sur elle.

Nn

mouth   la bouche

la bouche —

mushroom   le champignon

name   le nom

move   déplacer

Tom and Ian **move** the parcel.   Tom et Ian **déplacent** le paquet.

music   la musique

naughty   vilain

This dog is **naughty**.

Ce chien est **vilain**.

near — près

The tractor is near the wall. — Le tracteur est près du mur.

need — avoir besoin

Sam needs boots today.

Sam a besoin de bottes aujourd'hui.

nest — le nid

a bird's nest — un nid d'oiseaux

neck — le cou

le cou

needle — l'aiguille (f)

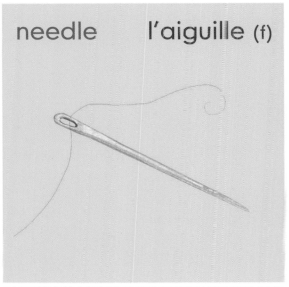

net — le filet

a fishing net

un filet de pêche

necklace — le collier

neighbour — le voisin

They are neighbours. — Ils sont voisins

never — jamais

Never play with matches.

Ne joue jamais avec les allumettes.

m
n

new **neuf** (m), **neuve** (f)

a **new** bag — un sac **neuf**

nobody **personne**

Nobody lives here.
Personne n'habite ici.

not **ne...pas**

He is **not** feeling well.
Il **ne** se sent **pas** bien.

newspaper **le journal**

noise **le bruit**

Babies make a lot of **noise**. Les bébés font beaucoup de **bruit**.

Waa! Waa!

Ouin ! Ouin !

nothing **rien**

There's **nothing** in the box. Il n'y a **rien** dans la boîte.

night **la nuit**

a starry **night** — une **nuit** étoilée

nose **le nez**

le nez

now **maintenant**

There are four children **now**.
Il y a quatre enfants **maintenant**.

number le chiffre, le numéro, le nombre

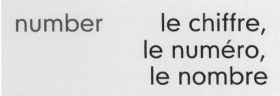

5

This is the **number** five.
Voici le **chiffre** cinq.

Oo

of de

a piece **of** cake

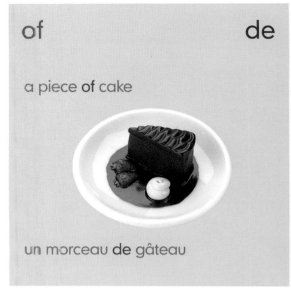

un morceau **de** gâteau

nurse l'infirmier (m), l'infirmière (f)

o'clock heure (f), heures

three **o'clock** in the afternoon

trois **heures** de l'après-midi

often souvent

She **often** takes Spot for a walk.

Elle promène **souvent** Spot.

nut*

a walnut
une noix

some **hazelnuts**
des **noisettes**

some **peanuts**
des **cacahuètes**

octopus la pieuvre

oil l'huile (f)

* In French, there is no word for **nut**. There are only words for different kinds of nuts.

old — vieux (m), vieil (m), vieille (f)

an old woman and an old man

une vieille femme et un vieil homme

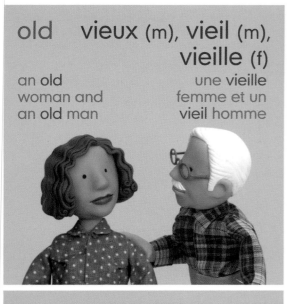

only — seulement

The orange cat has **only** one cushion.

Le chat orange a **seulement** un coussin.

orange — l'orange (f)

once — une fois

He takes a shower **once** a day.

Il prend une douche **une fois** par jour.

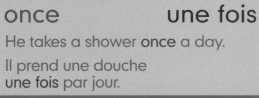

open — ouvrir

Alice **opens** the door.

Alice **ouvre** la porte.

other — l'autre (m/f)

Where is the **other** sock?

Où est l'autre chaussette ?

onion — l'oignon (m)

or — ou

Do you want pasta **or** soup?

Vous voulez des pâtes **ou** de la soupe ?

owl — le hibou

O
P

Pp

palace   le palais

park   le parc

page   la page

She's turning the page.   Elle tourne la page.

panda   le panda

party   la fête

paint   peindre

She is painting.

Elle peint.

paper   le papier

He's folding some paper.   Il plie du papier.

pasta   les pâtes (f)

o
p

| peach — la pêche | pen — le stylo | people — les gens (m/f) |

peach — **la pêche**

pen — **le stylo**

three **pens** — trois **stylos**

people — **les gens** (m/f)

There are lots of **people** at the market. — Il y a beaucoup de **gens** au marché.

pear — **la poire**

pencil — **le crayon**

pet — **l'animal domestique** (m)

some **pets**

des **animaux domestiques**

peas — **les petits pois** (m)

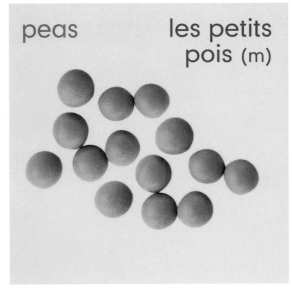

penguin — **le manchot**

piano — **le piano**

P

picnic   le pique-nique

pillow   l'oreiller (m)

plane   l'avion (m)

picture   l'image (f)

pirate   le pirate

These children are dressed as pirates.   Ces enfants sont déguisés en pirates.

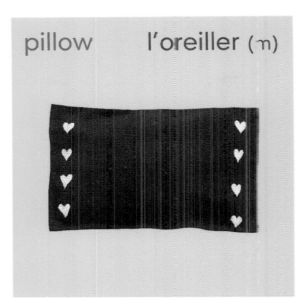

plant   la plante

piece   le morceau, les morceaux

a piece of cake   un morceau de gâteau

pizza   la pizza

plate   l'assiette (f)

There's food on this plate.

Il y a de la nourriture dans cette assiette.

p

play   jouer

They **are playing** together.

Ils **jouent** ensemble.

pocket   la poche

The boy is putting his hands in his **pockets**.

Le garçon met ses mains dans ses **poches**.

present   le cadeau, les cadeaux

lots of **presents**

beaucoup de **cadeaux**

playground   la cour de récréation, l'aire de jeux (f)

police officer   le policier, le gendarme

pretty   joli

These flowers are **pretty**.

Ces fleurs sont **jolies**.

plum   la prune

potato   la pomme de terre

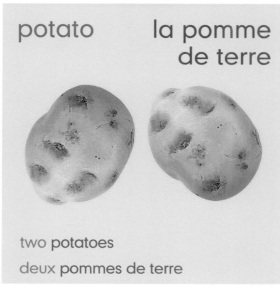

two **potatoes**

deux **pommes de terre**

princess   la princesse

P
Q

prize — le prix

The **prize** is a silver cup.

Le **prix** est une coupe en argent.

puppy — le chiot

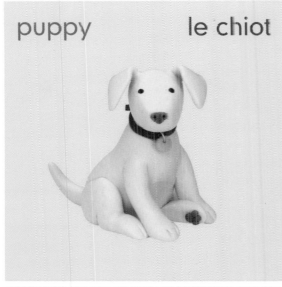

Qq

pull — tirer

The boy **pulls** the donkey.

Le garçon **tire** l'âne.

push — pousser

This girl is **pushing** her doll in a pushchair.

Cette fille **pousse** sa poupée dans une poussette.

queen — la reine

puppet — la marionnette

put (down) — poser

She **puts** the baby **down**.

Elle **pose** le bébé.

quiet — silencieux (m), silencieuse (f)

The baby is **quiet**.

Le bébé est **silencieux**.

Rr

rain   la pluie

rat   le rat

rabbit   le lapin

rainbow

l'arc-en-ciel (m)

read   lire

Tia enjoys **reading**.   Tia aime **lire**.

radio   la radio

raspberry

la framboise

some
raspberries

des
framboises

remember

se rappeler

A list
helps you
remember
what to
buy.

Une liste,
ça aide à
se rappeler
ce qu'il faut
acheter.

R

rice   le riz

river   la rivière

A river runs through the town.

Une rivière traverse la ville.

rocket   la fusée

ride   monter à cheval

Emily likes riding.

Emily aime monter à cheval.

road   la route

They are crossing the road.

Ils traversent la route.

roof   le toit

a red roof   un toit rouge

ring   la bague

three rings   trois bagues

robot   le robot

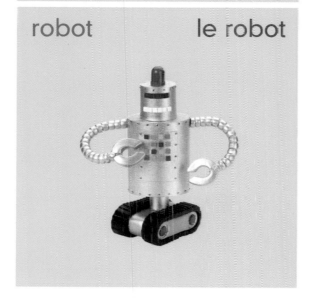

room   la pièce

This house has seven rooms.

Cette maison a sept pièces.

r

rope	la corde

Ss

sandwich	le sandwich

round	rond

a **round** ball   un ballon **rond**

sad	triste

This little boy looks **sad**.

Ce petit garçon a l'air **triste**.

say	dire

This woman **says**
she's lost her dog.

Cette femme **dit** qu'elle
a perdu son chien.

run	courir

The dogs **run** fast.

Les chiens **courent** vite.

sand	le sable

They are playing in the **sand**.
Ils jouent sur le **sable**.

scarf	l'écharpe (f)

R
S

| school | l'école (f) | secret | le secret | share | partager |

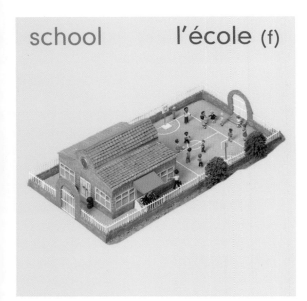

They are sharing some fruit.

Emily tells Lucy a **secret**.

Emily dit un **secret** à Lucy.

Elles **partagent** des fruits.

scissors — les ciseaux (m)

see — voir

The firefighter **sees** a dog.

Le pompier **voit** un chien.

sheep — le mouton

sea — la mer

sell — vendre

She **sells** fruit.

Elle **vend** des fruits.

ship — le navire

r
s

shoes
les chaussures (f)

show · montrer

Polly **shows** her dad her toy.

Polly **montre** son jouet à son papa.

sister · la sœur

two **sisters** · deux **sœurs**

short · court

This girl has **short** hair.

Cette fille a les cheveux **courts**.

silver · l'argent (m)

a **silver** necklace

un collier en **argent**

sit · être assis

They **are sitting**. · Ils **sont assis**.

shout · crier

Tom and Luke **are shouting**.

FIDO ! FIDO !

Tom et Luke **crient**.

sing · chanter

Annie loves **singing**.

Annie aime **chanter**.

skin · la peau

This boy's **skin** is pink.

La **peau** de ce garçon est rose.

S

skirt — la jupe

slow — lent

Tortoises are very slow.

Les tortues sont très lentes.

smile — sourire

They are smiling.

Ils sourient.

sky — le ciel

Planes fly in the sky.

Les avions volent dans le ciel.

small — petit

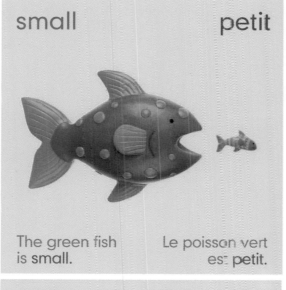

The green fish is small.

Le poisson vert est petit.

snail — l'escargot (m)

sleep — dormir

He wants to sleep.

Il veut dormir.

smell — sentir

The cat can smell the fish.

Le chat sent le poisson.

snake — le serpent

S

| snow | la neige | sofa | le canapé | spider | l'araignée (f) |

These cats are sitting on the sofa.

Ces chats sont assis sur le canapé.

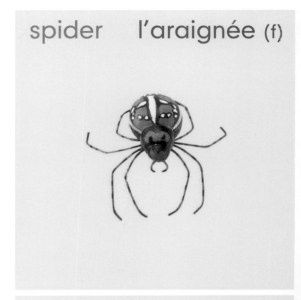

so **tellement**

She is so surprised.

Elle est **tellement** surprise.

soft **doux** (m), **douce** (f)

a **soft** blanket

une couverture **douce**

spoon **la cuillère**

soap **le savon**

some **du** (m), **de la** (f), **des** (plural)

some bread
some flour
some eggs

du pain
de la farine
des œufs

stand **être debout**

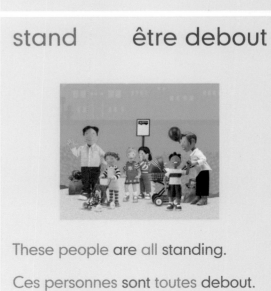

These people are all standing.

Ces personnes sont toutes debout.

star   l'étoile (f)

shiny stars
des étoiles brillantes

story   l'histoire (f)

a story about firefighters

une histoire sur les pompiers

sun   le soleil

start   commencer

The party starts at 3 o'clock.

La fête commence à trois heures.

strawberry   la fraise

supermarket
le supermarché

stop   s'arrêter

Cars have to stop here.

Les voitures doivent s'arrêter ici.

street   la rue

swim   nager

This boy loves swimming.
Ce garçon aime nager.

S

Tt

take — prendre

He takes the box. — Il prend la boîte.

teacher — l'instituteur (m), l'institutrice (f)

table — la table

talk — parler

They are talking together. — Elles parlent ensemble.

teddy bear — le nounours

tail — la queue
The dog is wagging his tail.

Le chien remue sa queue.

tall — grand
Emily is tall for her age.

Emily est grande pour son âge.

teeth — les dents (f)
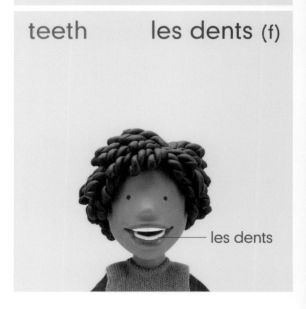
les dents

T

telephone
le téléphone

He is on the telephone.

Il est au téléphone.

throw lancer

He is throwing a snowball.

Il lance une boule de neige.

time l'heure (f)

What time is it?

Quelle heure est-il ?

television
la télévision

thumb le pouce

le pouce

tired fatigué

He is very tired.

Il est très fatigué.

thing la chose

There are lots of things on the table.

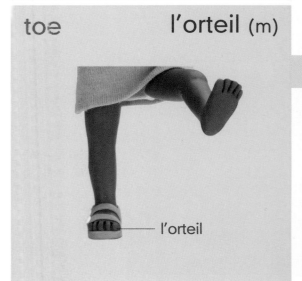

Il y a beaucoup de choses sur la table.

tiger le tigre

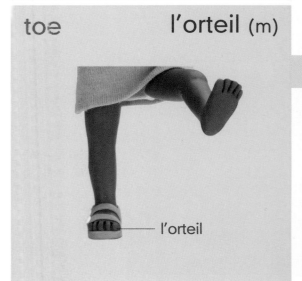

toe l'orteil (m)

l'orteil

t

tomato — la tomate	town — la ville	train — le train

tomato   la tomate

town   la ville

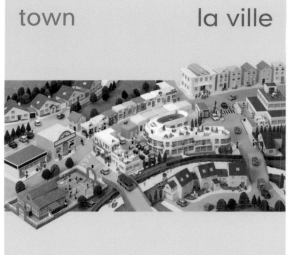

train   le train

tongue   la langue

— la langue

toy   le jouet

tree   l'arbre (m)

towel   la serviette

tractor   le tracteur

truck   le camion

U u

ugly — laid

This fish is ugly.

Ce poisson est laid.

umbrella — le parapluie

V v

vase — le vase

a vase of flowers

un vase de fleurs

vegetables — les légumes (m)

very — très

Firefighters are very brave.

Les pompiers sont très courageux.

visit — visiter

A clown is visiting Paul's house.

Un clown visite la maison de Paul.

voice — la voix

Ww

walk **marcher**

The boy **walks** with his mum.

Le garçon **marche** avec sa maman.

warm **chaud**

warm clothes

des vêtements **chauds**

wait **attendre**

They **are** all **waiting**.

Ils **attendent** tous.

wall **le mur**

They are building a **wall**.

Ils construisent un **mur**.

wash **se laver**

He **is washing** himself.

Il **se lave**.

wake up **se réveiller**

It's time to **wake up**!

Il est l'heure de **se réveiller** !

want **vouloir**

The puppy **wants** to play.

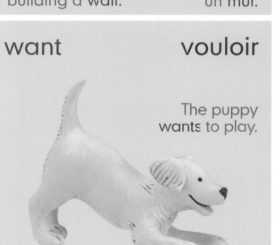

Le chiot **veut** jouer.

watch **la montre**

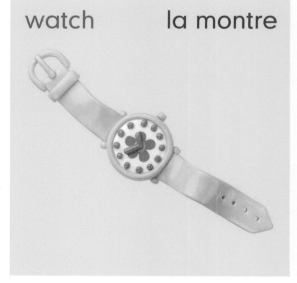

W

water   **l'eau** (f)

wet   **mouillé**

This man is all wet!

Cet homme est tout mouillé !

whisper   **chuchoter**

The boy is whispering.

Le garçon chuchote.

wave   **saluer**

They are waving to their friends.

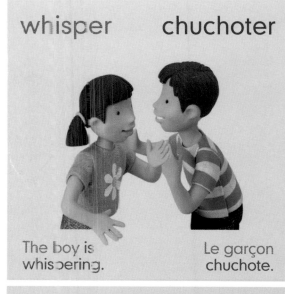

Ils saluent leurs amis.

whale   **la baleine**

win   **gagner**

Who is winning?

Qui gagne ?

wear   **porter**

Chefs wear hats.

Les chefs cuisiniers portent des chapeaux.

wheel   **la roue**

window   **la fenêtre**

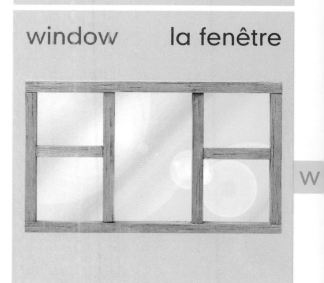

W

wing   l'aile (f)

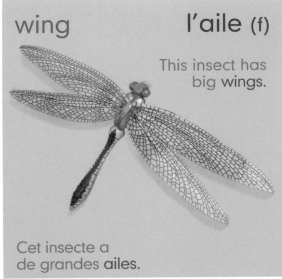

This insect has big wings.

Cet insecte a de grandes ailes.

work   travailler

They **work** in a restaurant.

Ils **travaillent** dans un restaurant.

Xx

with   avec

Amy is **with** her mum.

Amy est **avec** sa maman.

worm   le ver de terre

x-ray   la radio

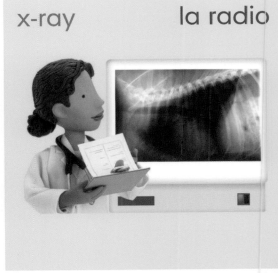

woman   la femme

write   écrire

She **is writing** her name.

Elle **écrit** son nom.

xylophone   le xylophone

Yy

yet   **encore**

This baby can't walk **yet**.

Ce bébé ne sait pas encore marcher.

yawn   **bâiller**

He is **yawning**.

Il bâille.

yogurt   **le yaourt**

year   **l'année (f), l'an (m)**

This girl is seven **years** old.

Cette fille a sept **ans**.

young   **jeune**

A foal is a **young** horse.   Un poulain est un **jeune** cheval.

Zz

zebra   **le zèbre**

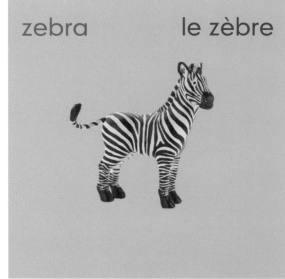

zip   **la fermeture éclair**

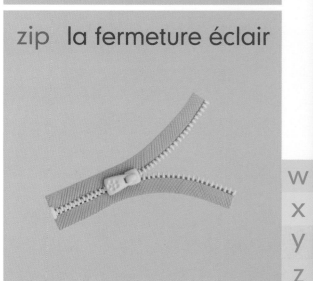

Where are they?

Où sont-ils ?

These two pages show some words you use when you want to say where someone or something is.

behind — derrière

Andrew is behind Lola.

Andrew est derrière Lola.

in — dans

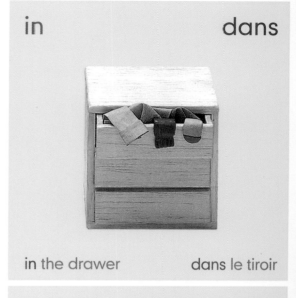

in the drawer — dans le tiroir

above — au-dessus de

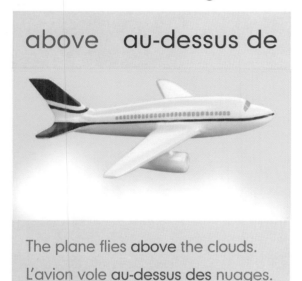

The plane flies above the clouds.

L'avion vole au-dessus des nuages.

between — entre

Sam is between two grown-ups.

Sam est entre deux grandes personnes.

in front of — devant

The cars are in front of the house.

Les voitures sont devant la maison.

around — autour de

They are sitting around the table.

Ils sont assis autour de la table.

here/there — ici/là-bas

I'm here, he's over there.

Je suis ici, il est là-bas.

inside — dedans, à l'intérieur

There are people inside.

Il y a des gens à l'intérieur.

into   dans

Ann puts the duckling **into** the pond.

Ann met le poussin **dans** la mare.

opposite   en face de

Tom is sitting **opposite** Leah.

Tom est assis **en face de** Leah.

to/from   à/de

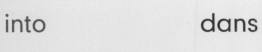

Anna goes **from** her house **to** school by bus.

Anna va **de** sa maison **à** l'école en bus.

next to   à côté de

Patch is sitting **next to** Ted.

Patch est assis **à côté de** Ted.

outside   dehors

These people are **outside**.

Ces personnes sont **dehors**.

under   sous

under the table   **sous** la table

on   sur

The girl is lying **on** the doctor's table.

La fille est allongée **sur** la table du médecin.

over   au-dessus de

The lamb jumps **over** the flowers.

L'agneau saute **au-dessus** des fleurs.

up/down

en haut/en bas

One girl goes **up** when the other is **down**.

Une fille va **en haut** quand l'autre est **en bas**.

I, you, he, she
Je, tu, il, elle

This page shows some words you use when you want to talk about yourself, other people or things.

he — il

He has a sister.   Il a une sœur.

we — nous

We each have a bag.

Nous avons chacune un sac.

I — je, j'

I have a brother.   J'ai un frère.

she — elle

She has a doll.   Elle a une poupée.

you — vous

Are you all sitting?

Êtes-vous tous assis ?

you — tu

Do you know the answer?

Est-ce que tu connais la réponse ?

it — il (m), elle (f)

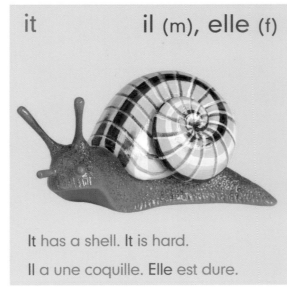

It has a shell. It is hard.

Il a une coquille. Elle est dure.

they — ils (m), elles (f)

They have lots of dogs.
They are all very cute.

Elles ont beaucoup de chiens.
Ils sont tous très mignons.

Questions
Les questions

This page shows some
of the words you can use
when you want to ask a
question about something.

what — qu'est-ce que

What
are you
reading?

Qu'est-ce
que tu lis ?

which — quel (m), quelle (f)

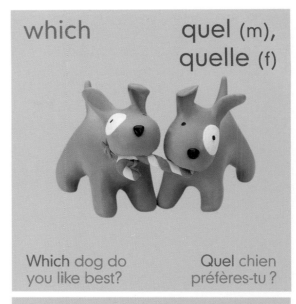

Which dog do
you like best?

Quel chien
préfères-tu ?

how — comment

How do you
make a cake?

Comment fais-tu
un gâteau ?

when — quand

When does the bus arrive?

Quand arrive le bus ?

who — qui

Who is singing?   Qui chante ?

how many — combien

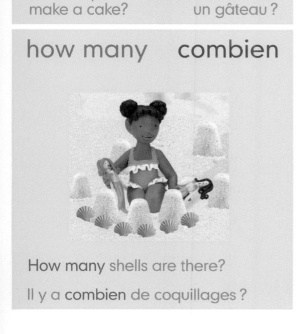

How many shells are there?

Il y a combien de coquillages ?

where — où

Where are
my friends?

Où sont
mes amis ?

why — pourquoi

Why is
Laura sad?

Pourquoi est-ce que Laura est triste ?

Colours Les couleurs (f)

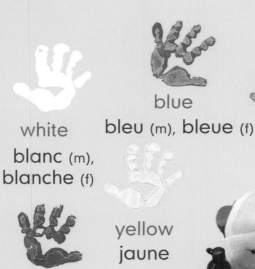

white
blanc (m),
blanche (f)

blue
bleu (m), **bleue** (f)

yellow
jaune

pink
rose

purple
violet (m),
violette (f)

green
vert (m),
verte (f)

red
rouge

black
noir (m),
noire (f)

orange
orange

grey
gris (m), **grise** (f)

brown
marron

Shapes Les formes (f)

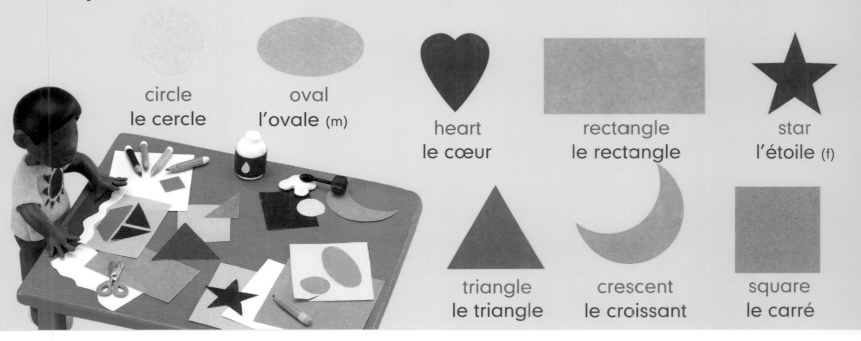

circle
le cercle

oval
l'ovale (m)

heart
le cœur

rectangle
le rectangle

star
l'étoile (f)

triangle
le triangle

crescent
le croissant

square
le carré

Numbers · Les nombres (m)

one	un	
two	deux	
three	trois	
four	quatre	
five	cinq	
six	six	
seven	sept	
eight	huit	
nine	neuf	
ten	dix	

Months
Les mois (m)

January	janvier
February	février
March	mars
April	avril
May	mai
June	juin
July	juillet
August	août
September	septembre
October	octobre
November	novembre
December	décembre

Days
Les jours (m)

Monday	lundi
Tuesday	mardi
Wednesday	mercredi
Thursday	jeudi
Friday	vendredi
Saturday	samedi
Sunday	dimanche

Seasons
Les saisons (f)

spring	le printemps
summer	l'été (m)
autumn	l'automne (m)
winter	l'hiver (m)

Using your dictionary

When you have looked up a word, here are some things you can find out.

drink   la boisson

a cold drink   une **boisson** fraîche

You can see the French translation of the word.

You can see a picture of the word, or a way of using the word.

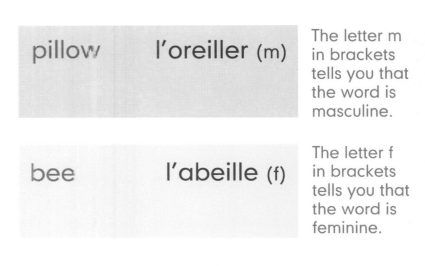

pillow   l'oreiller (m)

The letter m in brackets tells you that the word is masculine.

bee   l'abeille (f)

The letter f in brackets tells you that the word is feminine.

Masculine or feminine?

In French, all nouns, or "naming" words such as "boy" and "house", are either masculine or feminine. The French word for "the" is <u>le</u> for masculine nouns and <u>la</u> for feminine words. The French word for "a" or "an" is <u>un</u> for masculine nouns and <u>une</u> for feminine nouns.

Sometimes you can guess whether a noun is feminine or masculine – for example, "boy" is masculine (le garçon). Other times, you need to check the dictionary.

If a noun begins with a, e, i, o, or u, and sometimes h, then le or la is shortened to <u>l'</u>.

Plurals

"Plural" means "more than one". The French for "the" when you are talking about more than one is <u>les</u>, for both masculine and feminine nouns. You also add <u>s</u> at the end of the noun, as you do in English:

boy   le garçon
boys   les garçons

If the noun ends in s already, you don't need to add another s:

mouse   la souris
mice   les souris

A few nouns have a different spelling in the plural.

horse   le cheval, les chevaux

Nouns with a different plural are shown like this.

Adjectives

"Describing" words, such as "small", "cold" or "happy", are adjectives.

In English, an adjective is always spelled the same, whatever it is describing. In French, the endings of an adjective change, depending on whether the noun is feminine or masculine, singular or plural.

For example, the French word for "hot" is "chaud":

a hot bath   un bain chaud

For a feminine noun, you add <u>e</u> to the end of the adjective (unless it ends in e already):

hot water   l'eau chaude

For masculine plurals, you add <u>s</u> to the end of the adjective (unless it ends in s or x already):

hot dishes   les plats chauds

For feminine plurals, you add <u>es</u>:

hot drinks   les boissons chaudes

A few adjectives have slightly different feminine forms. They are shown in the dictionary like this:

good	bon (m), bonne (f)
long	long (m), longue (f)

A very few adjectives also have a different form before masculine nouns beginning with a, e, i, o, u, and sometimes h. They are shown like this:

old	vieux (m), vieil (m), vieille (f)
an old cat	un vieux chat
an old donkey	un vieil âne
an old woman	une vieille femme

In English, adjectives usually go before the noun they are describing. In French, most adjectives go after the noun:

a blue flower	une fleur bleue
a soft blanket	une couverture douce

A few very common adjectives go before the noun they are describing:

a good book	un bon livre
a big garden	un grand jardin
a fat cat	un gros chat
a young child	un jeune enfant
a pretty flower	une jolie fleur
a long dress	une longue robe
a bad smell	une mauvaise odeur
a small boy	un petit garçon
an old house	une vieille maison
a naughty dog	un vilain chien

Verbs

"Doing" words, such as "walk" or "laugh", are called verbs. In English, verbs don't change very much, whoever is doing them:

I walk
you walk
he walks
she walks
we walk
you walk
they walk

In French, the endings change much more. Many verbs work in a similar way to the one below. The verb is in the present – the form you use to talk about what's happening now.

to give	donner
I give	je donne
you give*	tu donnes
he gives	il donne
she gives	elle donne
we give	nous donnons
you give*	vous donnez
they give	ils donnent
	elles donnent

When you look up a verb in the dictionary, you will find the "to" form, together with a sentence or phrase that shows how the verb can be used. All these sentences use the verb in the present form.

Two useful verbs

Two of the most useful verbs to know are "to be" and "to have". Here they are in French, in the present form:

to be	être
I am	je suis
you are*	tu es
he is	il est
she is	elle est
we are	nous sommes
you are*	vous êtes
they are	ils sont
	elles sont

to have	avoir
I have	j'ai
you have*	tu as
he has	il a
she has	elle a
we have	nous avons
you have*	vous avez
they have	ils ont
	elles ont

Mostly, you use them in just the same way as you do in English:

I have a sister.	J'ai une sœur.
She is tall.	Elle est grande.

Just sometimes, it isn't the verb you expect:

I am eight.	J'ai huit ans.

* In French, you use "tu" for one person, either a young person or someone you know well. You use "vous" for more than one person, or for an older person or someone you don't know very well.

French word list

French	English	French	English
à	at, to	l'année (f)	year
à côté de	next to	l'anniversaire (m)	birthday
à l'intérieur	inside	août	August
l'abeille (f)	bee	après	after
acheter	to buy	l'après-midi (m)	afternoon
l'agneau (m)	lamb	l'araignée (f)	spider
aider	to help	l'arbre (m)	tree
l'aigle (m)	eagle	l'arc-en-ciel (m)	rainbow
l'aiguille (f)	needle	l'argent (m)	money, silver
l'aile (f)	wing	s'arrêter	to stop
aimer	to like, to love	l'assiette (f)	plate
l'air (m), les airs (m)	air	l'astronaute (m/f)	astronaut
l'aire de jeux (f)	playground	attendre	to wait
aller	to go	attraper	to catch
l'alphabet (m)	alphabet	au-dessus de	above, over
l'ambulance (f)	ambulance	l'autobus (m)	bus
l'ami (m), l'amie (f)	friend	l'automne (m)	autumn
l'an (m)	year	autour de	around
l'âne (m)	donkey	l'autre (m/f)	other
l'ange (m)	angel	avec	with
l'animal (m)	animal	l'avion (m)	plane
l'animal domestique (m)	pet	avoir besoin	to need

avril	April	la boue	mud
la bague	ring	le bout	end
bâiller	to yawn	le bouton	button
le bain	bath	le bras	arm
le baiser	kiss	la brosse	brush
la baleine	whale	le bruit	noise
la balle	ball	le bus	bus
le ballon	ball	la cacahuète	peanut
la banane	banana	se cacher	to hide
la barrière	gate	le cadeau	present
le bateau	boat	le camion	truck
beaucoup	a lot, lots	le canapé	sofa
le bébé	baby	le canard	duck
la bicyclette	bicycle	la capuche	hood
les bijoux (m)	jewellery	la carotte	carrot
blanc (m), blanche (f)	white	le carré	square
bleu	blue	la carte	map, card
la boisson	drink	la ceinture	belt
la boîte	box	le cercle	circle
le bol	bowl	le cerf-volant	kite
bon (m), bonne (f)	good	la cerise	cherry
les bottes (f)	boots	la chaise	chair
la bouche	mouth	le champignon	mushroom
la bouchée	bite	chanter	to sing

le chapeau	hat	la coccinelle	ladybird
chaque	each	le cochon d'Inde	guinea pig
le chat	cat	le cœur	heart
le château	castle	le collier	necklace
le chaton	kitten	combien	how many, how much
chaud	warm, hot	commencer	to start
les chaussures (f)	shoes	comment	how
le cheval	horse	conduire	to drive
les cheveux (m)	hair	construire	to build
la cheville	ankle	la corde	rope
la chèvre	goat	le cou	neck
le chien	dog	le coude	elbow
le chiffre	number	la couleur	colour
le chiot	puppy	la cour de récréation	playground
le chocolat	chocolate	courir	to run
la chose	thing	court	short
chuchoter	to whisper	le couteau	knife
le ciel	sky	la couverture	blanket
cinq	five	le crayon	pencil
les ciseaux (m)	scissors	creuser	to dig
le citron	lemon	crier	to shout
clair	light	le croissant	crescent
la clé	key	la cuillère	spoon
la clef	key	la cuisine	kitchen

dans	in, into	le doigt	finger
danser	to dance	donner	to give
de	of, from	donner un coup de pied	to kick
de la (f)	any, some	dormir	to sleep
décembre	December	doux (m), douce (f)	soft
dedans	inside	le dragon	dragon
dehors	outside	le drapeau	flag
le déjeuner	lunch	du (m)	any, some
demander	to ask	dur	hard
démanger	to itch	l'eau (f)	water
le/la dentiste	dentist	l'écharpe (f)	scarf
les dents (f)	teeth	l'école (f)	school
déplacer	to move	écouter	to listen
derrière	behind	écrire	to write
des (plural)	any, some	l'éléphant (m)	elephant
le désordre	mess	elle	she, it
dessiner	to draw	elles	they (f)
deux	two	embrasser	to hug
devant	in front of	l'emploi (m)	work, job
dimanche	Sunday	en bas	down
le dinosaure	dinosaur	en face de	opposite
dire	to say	en haut	up
dix	ten	encore	again, yet, another
le docteur	doctor	l'encre (f)	ink

endormi	asleep	la fête	party
entendre	to hear	le feu	fire
entre	between	la feuille	leaf
l'escargot (m)	snail	février	February
est	is	le filet	net
l'été (m)	summer	la fille	girl
l'étoile (f)	star	la fleur	flower
être assis	to sit	la forêt	forest
être couché	to lie	les formes (f)	shapes
être debout	to stand	fort	loud, strong
éveillé	awake	la fourchette	fork
fâché	angry	la fourmi	ant
faire	to do, to make	la fraise	strawberry
faire la cuisine	to cook	la framboise	raspberry
faire mal	to hurt	frapper	to hit
la famille	family	le frère	brother
le fantôme	ghost	froid	cold
fatigué	tired	le fromage	cheese
la fée	fairy	les fruits (m)	fruit
la femme	woman	la fusée	rocket
la fenêtre	window	gagner	to win
le fer à repasser	iron	les gants (m)	gloves
la ferme	farm	le garçon	boy
la fermeture éclair	zip	le gâteau	cake

le géant	giant	huit	eight
le gendarme	police officer	ici	here
le genou	knee	l'idée (f)	idea
les gens (m/f)	people	il	he, it
la girafe	giraffe	l'île (f)	island
la glace	ice, ice cream, mirror	ils	they (m)
grand	big, tall	l'image (f)	picture
la grande personne	grown-up	l'infirmier (m), l'infirmière (f)	nurse
la grenouille	frog	l'insecte (m)	insect
gris	grey	l'instituteur (m), l'institutrice (f)	teacher
gros (m), grosse (f)	fat	l'invitation (f)	invitation
habiter	to live	jamais	never
le hamster	hamster	la jambe	leg
l'hélicoptère (m)	helicopter	janvier	January
l'herbe (f)	grass	le jardin	garden
l'heure (f)	time, o'clock	jaune	yellow
heureux (m), heureuse (f)	happy	je, j'	I
le hibou	owl	le jean, les jeans	jeans
hier	yesterday	le jeu	game
l'histoire (f)	story	jeudi	Thursday
l'hiver (m)	winter	jeune	young
l'homme (m)	man	joli	pretty
l'hôpital (m)	hospital	jongler	to juggle
l'huile (f)	oil	jouer	to play

73

le jouet	toy	lire	to read
le jour	day	le lit	bed
le journal	newspaper	le livre	book
juillet	July	long (m), longue (f)	long
juin	June	lundi	Monday
la jungle	jungle	la lune	moon
la jupe	skirt	les lunettes (f)	glasses
le jus	juice	la machine	machine
le kangourou	kangaroo	la magie	magic
le ketchup	ketchup	mai	May
là-bas	there	la main	hand
laid	ugly	maintenant	now
laisser	to let	la maison	house, home
le lait	milk	le manchot	penguin
la lampe	lamp	manger	to eat
lancer	to throw	le manteau	coat
la langue	tongue	marcher	to walk
le lapin	rabbit	mardi	Tuesday
se laver	to wash	la marionnette	puppet
les légumes (m)	vegetables	marron	brown
lent	slow	mars	March
la lettre	letter	le matin	morning
les lèvres (f)	lips	mauvais	bad
le lion	lion	le médecin	doctor

la mer	sea	noir	black, dark
mercredi	Wednesday	la noisette	hazelnut
le miel	honey	la noix	walnut
le miroir	mirror	le nom	name
le mois	month	le nombre	number
le monstre	monster	le nounours	teddy bear
la montagne	mountain	la nourriture	food
monter à cheval	to ride (a horse)	nous	we
la montre	watch	novembre	November
montrer	to show	le nuage	cloud
le morceau	piece	la nuit	night
la moto	motorbike	le numéro	number
mouillé	wet	octobre	October
le mouton	sheep	l'œil (m)	eye
le mur	wall	l'œuf (m)	egg
la musique	music	l'oie (f)	goose
nager	to swim	l'oignon (m)	onion
le navire	ship	l'oiseau (m)	bird
ne...pas	not	l'or (m)	gold
la neige	snow	orange	orange (colour)
neuf	nine	l'orange (f)	orange (fruit)
neuf (m), neuve (f)	new	l'ordinateur (m)	computer
le nez	nose	l'oreille (f)	ear
le nid	nest	l'oreiller (m)	pillow

l'orteil (m)	toe	la pendule	clock
l'os (m)	bone	personne	nobody
ou	or	petit	little, small
où	where	le petit déjeuner (m)	breakfast
l'ours (m)	bear	les petits pois (m)	peas
ouvrir	to open	le piano	piano
l'ovale (m)	oval	la pièce	room
la page	page	le pied	foot
le pain	bread	la pierre précieuse	jewel
le palais	palace	la pieuvre	octopus
le panda	panda	le pique-nique	picnic
le panier	basket	le pirate	pirate
le papier	paper	la pizza	pizza
le papillon	butterfly	la plage	beach
le parapluie	umbrella	la plante	plant
le parc	park	pleurer	to cry
parler	to talk	la pluie	rain
partager	to share	plus	more
les pâtes (f)	pasta	la poche	pocket
la peau	skin	la poire	pear
la pêche	peach	le poisson	fish
peindre	to paint	le poisson rouge	goldfish
la pelleteuse	digger	le policier	police officer
la pelouse	grass	la pomme	apple

la pomme de terre	potato	la question	question
le pompier	firefighter	la queue	tail, queue
la porte	door	qui	who
porter	to wear, to carry	la radio	radio, x-ray
poser	to put (down)	le raisin	grapes
le pot	jar	se rappeler	to remember
le pouce	thumb	le rat	rat
le poulet	chicken	le rectangle	rectangle
la poupée	doll	regarder	to look (at)
pourquoi	why	la reine	queen
pousser	to push, to grow	le renard	fox
pouvoir	can, to be able to	réveillé	awake
prendre	to take	se réveiller	to wake up
près	near	rien	nothing
la princesse	princess	rire	to laugh
le printemps	spring	la rivière	river
le prix	prize, price	le riz	rice
profond	deep	la robe	dress
la prune	plum	le robot	robot
le puzzle	jigsaw puzzle	le roi	king
quand	when	rond	round
quatre	four	rose	pink
quel (m), quelle (f)	which	la roue	wheel
qu'est-ce que	what	rouge	red

la route	road	six	six
la rue	street	la sœur	sister
le sable	sand	le sol	floor
le sac	bag	le soleil	sun
la saison	season	sont	are
sale	dirty	sourire	to smile
saluer	to wave	la souris	mouse
samedi	Saturday	sous	under
le sandwich	sandwich	souvent	often
sauter	to jump	le stylo	pen
sauter à cloche-pied	to hop	le supermarché	supermarket
le savon	soap	sur	on, about
sec (m), sèche (f)	dry	la table	table
le secret	secret	le tambour	drum
sentir	to smell, to feel	la tasse	cup
sept	seven	le téléphone	telephone
septembre	September	la télévision	television
le serpent	snake	tellement	so
la serviette	towel	la Terre	Earth
seulement	only	la terre	ground
si	if	la tête	head
silencieux (m), silencieuse (f)	quiet	le tigre	tiger
le singe	monkey	tirer	to pull
la sirène	mermaid	le toit	roof

la tomate	tomato	les vêtements (m)	clothes
toujours	always	vide	empty
tout (m) (tous), toute (f) (toutes)	all	vieux (m), vieil (m), vieille (f)	old
le tracteur	tractor	vilain	naughty, ugly
le train	train	la ville	town
travailler	to work	violet (m), violette (f)	purple
très	very	le visage	face
le triangle	triangle	visiter	to visit
triste	sad	vite	fast
trois	three	voir	to see
le trou	hole	le voisin	neighbour
tu	you	la voiture	car
un (m), une (f)	a, an, one	la voiture de pompiers	fire engine
une fois	once	la voix	voice
la vache	cow	voler	to fly, to steal
le vase	vase	vouloir	to want
le vélo	bicycle	vous	you
vendre	to sell	le xylophone	xylophone
vendredi	Friday	le yaourt	yogurt
venir	to come	le zèbre	zebra
le ver de terre	worm		
le verre	glass		
vert	green		
la veste	jacket		

Hear the words on the internet

If you can use the internet and your computer can play sounds, you can listen to all the French words in this dictionary, read by a French person.

Go to the Usborne Quicklinks Website at www.usborne-quicklinks.com Type in the keywords **very first dictionary in french** and follow the simple instructions. Try listening to the words and then saying them yourself. This will help you learn to speak French easily and well. Always follow the safety rules on the right when you are using the internet.

What you need

To play the French words, your computer may need a small program called a media player, such as RealPlayer® or Windows® Media Player. These programs are free, and if you don't already have one, you can download a copy from www.usborne-quicklinks.com

Internet safety rules

Ask your parent's or guardian's permission before you connect to the internet and make sure you follow these simple rules:

• Never give out information about yourself, such as your real name, address, phone number or the name of your school.

• If a site asks you to log in or register by typing your name or email address, ask permission from an adult first.

Notes for parents or guardians

The Very First Dictionary area of the Usborne Quicklinks Website contains no links to external websites. However, other areas of Usborne Quicklinks do contain links to websites that do not belong to Usborne Publishing. The links are regularly reviewed and updated, but Usborne Publishing is not responsible, and does not accept liability, for the content or availability of any website other than its own, or for any exposure to harmful, offensive or inaccurate material which may appear on the Web.

We recommend that children are supervised while on the internet, that they do not use internet chat rooms and that you use internet filtering software to block unsuitable material. Please ensure that your children follow the safety guidelines above.

For more information, see the "Net Help" area of the Usborne Quicklinks Website at www.usborne-quicklinks.com

French language consultant: Lorraine Beurton-Sharp

Edited by Fiona Chandler

Additional design by Stephanie Jones

Photography by Howard Allman & MMStudios

With thanks to Paul Allen, Ben Denne and Sam Taplin, and to Staedtler UK for providing the Fimo® material for models. Vehicles supplied by Bruder® Toys.

RealPlayer is a trademark of RealNetworks, Inc., registered in the US and other countries.
Microsoft and Microsoft Windows are registered trademarks of Microsoft Corporation in the US and other countries.

First published in 2008 by Usborne Publishing Ltd., Usborne House, 83-85 Saffron Hill, London EC1N 8RT, England.
Copyright ©2008 Usborne Publishing Ltd.